Saint Ka

MW00974681

Review

a journal of poetry, fiction, creative non-fiction, and reviews

VOLUME 5 NUMBER 1

Poetry by
ROBERT CLAPS
ERIC POTTER
PAUL T. CORRIGAN
JILL PELÁEZ BAUMGAERTNER
TYLER KLINE
JACOB RIYEFF
BARBARA CROOKER
JOANNE ALLRED
STELLA NESANOVICH
DEVON MILLER-DUGGAN
AARON BROWN
CAMERON LAWRENCE
RAINA JOINES
MICHAEL D. RILEY
BRUCE BOND

Fiction by
ROBERT MCGUILL
ANGELA DOLL CARLSON

Nonfiction by
MARJORIE MADDOX
MARYANNE WILIMEK
MARY ANNE REESE

Inquiry Seeking Wisdom

Copyright © 2016 **Saint Katherine Review** Volume 5 Number 1
ISSN 2157-1759

Editorial Staff:

Editor | **Fr Kaleeg Hainsworth**
Managing Editor | **Gaelan Gilbert**
Nonfiction Editor | **TBA**
Poetry Editor | **Scott Cairns**
Fiction Editor | **TBA**
Founder | **Frank Papatheofanis**

Saint Katherine Review is published quarterly by University of Saint
Katherine Press, the publishing arm of University of Saint Katherine,
1637 Capalina Road, San Marcos, CA, 92069

Subscription Rates (U.S.):

Subscribe online at
stkathreview.org

One year (four issues): $39.99 for
individuals; $35.00 for institutions

Two years (eight issues): $59.99 for
individuals; $55.00 for institutions

Three years (12 issues): $79.99 for
individuals; $75.00 for institutions

Submissions:

All submissions should be submitted
via electronic mail to the appropriate
genre editors. Please see the University
of Saint Katherine Press web page
at www.stkath.org/skc-press for
addresses.

Advertising Rates:

Ad artwork must be submitted as a
600 ppi digital file.

Full page (5.25"w x 8.5"h): $300 each.

Half-page (5.25"w x 4.25"h): $200 each.

Contents

Poetry

Nature Poem with Recyclables

written by ROBERT CLAPS

October, at the flawless end to a year of I.E.D's
and suicide bombers, the grackles arrive in great
clusters to pepper these oak crowns, nodding
on a narrow strip between the interstate and the Price
Chopper parking lot, where we in the middle
Of our chores stop to listen: their shrill calls
Punctuated by the contrabass of the big rigs
Soaring into the unrelenting blue, morphing, I swear,
Into song. Even the sullen teenager gathering
Shopping carts strewn across the lot removes his
Ear buds and looks heavenward. The carts can wait.
Better to learn how to stand guard against despair,
than to busy ourselves otherwise, like that guy
dressed in camouflage and hauling black plastic bags
brimming with empties into the store for redemption.

Faith

written by ERIC POTTER

that stray dog, poking
its nose into everything,
turning up unannounced
and unwanted, distrustful
of crowds, always
loitering on the edge,
but never close enough
to pet, just a mutt
with bad teeth and worse
breath, limping along
half-wagging its stump,
no collar, no shots,
no registration,
won't roll over or fetch,
won't come when called,
though it may show up
at your back step
lean and hungry,
if you feed it table scraps
it might keep coming back,
if you chain it,
it might not stray again
but it won't be the same.

Story of the Northern Lights

written by PAUL T. CORRIGAN

—after Gabrielle Wu's *Iceland Revelations: Aurora upon the Vatnajokull*

One Inuit story attributes
The Northern Lights to people

Playing soccer in the sky,
Those who have passed on
Passing around a walrus head
For a ball.

Another has the walruses
Playing the game, kicking around
One of our skulls.

But, as you've surely been told, these lights
Have more to do with electromagnetics
Than with the souls of animals or the dead.

Science tends to deflate our stories.
Our mystical walruses,
Our spirits playing soccer in the sky.

Still, information isn't meaning.
So let us tell a new
Story of the *aurora borealis*.

Green, blue, and red dance
Against the dark sky
Above arctic glaciers and antarctic plains.

Just as we are changed upon our own first breath,
Particles from solar winds
Blown into earth's atmosphere

Are rewritten by oxygen
And, before our very eyes,
Give off light—

Exhibit

written by JILL PELÁEZ BAUMGAERTNER

Garfield Park Conservatory, 2002

1

Inside the translucent blue sphere
tiny cups catch the dew.

2

Globes of yellow glass streaked
vermillion, like slippery
buoys bob and drift
with the minute currents.

3

Azure worms spiral in and back,
cooling their color at stem ends
as they reach for light,
more light.

4

These among the spineless yucca,
the torch plants and purple
starfish flowers, the shrubby sea
bite and slipper spurge,
the giant carrion flowers,
the polka-dot euphorb.

5

And more—mouse ears, blood
bananas, prickly custard
apples and living baseballs
amidst Chihuly
rhombohedrons,
spikes and towers.
Which is glass?
Which stems and flowers?

Dinner Party

written by TYLER KLINE

After dinner we go to the porch for drinks.
In the field, Hanoverians idle along evening
like tall brown suits waiting the next train.
Insects have lost the sobriety of winter
and buzz about the horses' quarter-ton heads.

We walk down the rows. Plum tomatoes,
red coals that carry
sunset on their backs, drop from the vine.
Caterpillars necklace through flesh and palm,
leaving cursive letters.

We pass the Plymouth near the barn,
still as a defunct circus part.
Blue scalp chipping, seat-cushions losing humor,
hips sunken to the wet grass,
snake skin, one practice in losing, in the back seat –
no car should be a woman, not like this.
I raise a hand over the hood to feel what it once was:
metal heat, room for two anywhere,

cassette tape with the right notes,
brown-bottle-fire or something stronger every turn.
That engine block, large as a grandstand and once just as noisy,
sits like a mountain or resting gun, cold.
My friend tells me he could fix her and I nod,
leaving him to think he could.

Truth

written by JACOB RIYEFF

—A translation from Geoffrey Chaucer's *Truth or Ballade
de Bon Conseyl*

Flee the crowd and dwell securely in trueness.
Let your own suffice, though it not be much,
for greed leads to hate and grasping to coldness;
the crowd leads to envy, and wealth deceives such
as hold too tightly everything they touch.
Rule yourself well, that others may clearly see,
and have no doubt: the truth shall set you free.

Don't try to amend all that is amiss,
trusting in that Lady who spins like a ball;
true rest lies in spurning busyness.
There's no sense in kicking the point of an awl
nor in the crock's struggle against a wall.
Rule yourself, you who rule others' deeds,
and have no doubt: the truth shall set you free.

Take what is sent to you in obedience;
struggle for this world surely begs a fall.
We have no home here, only wilderness.
Go forth, pilgrim! Go forth, beast, from your stall!
Know our true home and thank the God of all.
Hold your course and follow your spirit's lead,
and have no doubt: the truth shall set you free.

The Alphabet

written by BARBARA CROOKER

So many open letters filled in with designs;
did the monks, like us, doodle all day?
There's an N made up of two wrestling men
that leads into the text about how no one can serve
two masters. Inside an H, there's a man whose lips help form
Jesus spoke. Two poor peacocks are squashed face-to-face
for eternity twined inside the letter U, while two hungry lions
become R and D, yoga for felines, ever-flexible. Imagine a P
made of cat, bird, and snake. Or a snake slithered into a knot,
hissing his name. For the monks, the very shapes of the letters
were magical, this graceful insular majuscule. Inscribed
with the simplest of materials, ink into hide, each initial
coils and curls, retraces the world in vegetal wonder.

Eve Explains The Soul's Genesis

written by JOANNE ALLRED

Driven out, I was driven in.
How else recover the unnamable lost?

Banished from the garden where every blossoming
reflected my image, I sought an un-fractured mirror.

Eden, Eve, we were one before I conceived
this separate self. The serpent held the looking glass

that split me. I was magnetized,
powerless to resist the milk letting down.

My nature flows toward hunger,
fresh possibility, an infant's cry.

My prayers invoking paradise,
songs recalling wildflowers

along the wayside, went unanswered. The calls
placed by mourning dove yearning from a tree

refused. I declined toward silence—
omnipresent want birthing the new world.

Sometimes Light

written by STELLA NESANOVICH

"Sometimes . . .a wave of light breaks into our darkness. . .."
—Paul Tillich, The Shaking of Foundations

The lights dimmed last night:
two lamps, one with a short,
another's switch quite stuck.
The ceiling kitchen fluorescence
also muted, and this morning
the bedroom lamp cast a paler glow.
My friend has brought two lamps
from Houston: one slender
with candle-shaped globes,
the other a blue ginger jar.

It's autumn. Outdoors, the sun's journey
south lessens the light. Evening descends
by five. December's gift of winter solstice
nears, as we celebrate with gifts, feasts,
and glitter. Today, we mark the pilgrim's
memorial with native peoples:
acorn squash, fowl, and yams.

Life presents a continuum: rituals
to honor those now gone.
Around me, I sense loved ones gather
as if for Eucharist, a communion,
as their souls seem to dart like angels,
their wings a flicker of light, movement
I glimpse as a shift of shade,
while outside, early this morning,
fog formed beads of moisture on screens
like stars in the night firmament.

I Made Things

written by DEVON MILLER-DUGGAN

It pleased that I was clever with my fingers—
drawings, elaborated eggshells, dolls, an evening gown for
    my mother—
so when I asked to have the feathers from a pheasant he'd hunted
he said he'd have them plucked for me to sort and use.

I don't know how to write about God except to count and
    sort the ways
I both believe and fail belief. As if I claimed to swim and couldn't,
but knew the salts would buoy me up
long enough to learn

Our car had hit a pheasant once. My father got out calmly,
    twisted its head
and body in different directions and explained the nature of
    kindness to me.
His hands were beautiful and skilled.
I'd thought I was the only thing he'd hurt.

I'd thought I'd get the feathers in a bag—an airy mass of
    flight and color.
Instead, the man who dressed his birds sent the whole skin
for me to pluck. I sorted every kind of feather into small bags.
The skin was supple in my hands.

My father knew I loathed his hunting. I liked that he knew.
I had things to make that wanted feathers.
He said he'd told the man to pluck the bird.
I don't recall it stank. He thought I'd chicken out.

One pheasant, if you take care, gives up feathers enough for fifty
    years of making
small things to give away.
I don't know how to speak of flight, except to count and sort the ways
I both loved and tore the bird.

Nasara

written by AARON BROWN

The word the kids would shout gleefully at the white boy
　walking down
　　their street; the same that would liquefy my limbs, make me notice

my skin, how it resembled more the sands baked by the sun
　than the warm earth richness of theirs—I wanted to chameleon

my way through the streets without being singled out as *nasara*,
　as foreigner, as other. The word that reminded me of what I was not.

The word that I did not understand until years later, a man, I leafed
　through the pages of a magazine, and saw the same word, nasara,

Nazarene, the first of its Arabic letters, nun, embossed on
　the cover page.
　　Reading how the letter was painted on the doors of Christians
　　in Iraq,

how militants would come back later to gather the flock and
　line them up
　　above a fresh-dug trench. The same word I read and had
　　to put down

to stare at the blinds, the way they only let in a fraction of light
even at midday, and I was chilled by the sense of a word

I was hearing as if for the first time, a meaning more for me
than it ever should have meant—the children wanting only

to see me turn and smile, those around me wanting only for me
to come and rest, to let go my words and let them join with theirs,

to dwell in the shade of language in a place beyond the past,
     where I sit,
with glossed pages lying bare and open, reading between their lines

a vision where another boy is taken out into the street, gun
     to his head,
     all because of that single word, nasara, meaning, *Christian.*

Progress Report

written by CAMERON LAWRENCE

I tried growing into one of the long-necked pines, their bearded
   heads in reverence nodding east, but stopped at the height
   of a man.

I searched an expanse of cave for the ancient still water, and washed
   myself in the earth's innocence.

I looked into the neverness of space between star and star and found
   gratitude for my existence.

I lay down on the ocean in hopes of learning to speak as a wave, in
   the language of wind traveling great distances, but my tongue
   couldn't make the sounds.

I stood over a crevasse with a bucket of coins and made a wish, one
   for each year I hoped to live.

I started a fire in the forest's undergrowth to witness freedom come
   into being at least once in my lifetime.

I floated on a melting sheet of ice in northern seas to remind myself
   time is running out.

I walked the desert from day's heat to cold of night and remembered
   the thirst is eternal.

Subtraction
written by RAINA JOINES

I

Crouching at his table,
a Japanese monk watches
as his master spoons rice into a bowl.
Their silent conversation
is a brief shuffle of one hand
against another: the movement
meaning enough. Each day,
enough is less
than the morning before,
until only the grain of the bowl remains,
curving around empty air.

II

Visiting physicists picnic on the steps.
Trying to rip a sandwich into portions,
they end up passing it around, griping
as rye crumbles into their books.
Even the still of a Florida afternoon
teems with humid flutter.
They argue about how to stop all movement
at the rim of a tube. Science moves
inside, to remove the largest numbers
from a pessimistic room. Each measurement
ruins an absolute zero.

Brendan

written by MICHAEL D. RILEY

—for Vicki Redpath

His name distils the
mystery he seeks.
Simplest architecture of a child's pen
held like a knife. Square lettered blocks open
to infinite sound—plastic, tough, and meek.
Approximate infinity his wild
birthright, Brendan the Navigator
lashed to his crayon, his imprimatur
crooked on the page, his body's child,
eyes, ears, skin, the home he calls his clothes.
Sailor of widest latitude and urge,
he caulks and bails but cannot drown the surge
he must open but cannot seem to close.
   He sails for home but cannot see the shore.
   He will learn to triangulate the star.

There

written by **BRUCE BOND**

—*after Jessica Murray*

And once I rowed out far enough to sea,
I paused. Be careful, love, the ocean said,
it's dangerous out there. It baffled me,
just how the sea could be here, this side
of there, and there where nobody could hear.
And I asked, Mother, are you in less pain,
now that you are no place in particular.
And the sea said nothing, and it went on
saying it, and my oars in their eyelets
knocked softly at the door of silence.
But there was no silence. Never is.
Only a pulse between my life and hers.
A sea-tide to pull me farther, deeper
in debt. The closing mist, my only shore.

Contributors

ROBERT CLAPS lives in eastern Connecticut, having retired from a career in information technology at the same company where Wallace Stevens had worked, though his abilities have not rubbed off on me. Soon he should be getting around to sending out a book length manuscript in hopes of publication. His poem "Jump Shots at Sixty" won **Sport Literate's** poetry competition for 2016. Other work has appeared in the **Green Mountains Review, The Connecticut River Review, The Hollins Critic**, and **The Atlanta Review**, among others. He has poems forthcoming in **Tar River Poetry**, and the **Louisville Review**. He is always reading new poets to hopefully fill the void in his life now that writers like Maxine Kumin, Galway Kinnell, and Philip Levine have passed away

ERIC POTTER is a professor of English at Grove City College (PA) where he teaches courses in modern poetry, American literature, and creative writing. His poetry has appeared in such publications as First Things, **The Christian Century**, and **Ruminate**, as well as in the anthology **Imago Dei: Poems from Christianity and Literature**. He is the author of two poetry chapbooks, **Heart Murmur and Still Life**, and a full-length collection, **Things Not Seen** (Wipf and Stock, 2015).

PAUL T. CORRIGAN teaches writing and literature at Southeastern University in Lakeland, Florida. He has published work in **Sewanee Theological Review, Christianity & Literature, Literature & Belief**, and other venues. His interview with Li-Young Lee recently appeared in Image. His dissertation at the University of South Florida, **Wrestling with Angels: Postsecular Contemporary American Poetry**, interprets contemporary poems that are spiritual or religious in nontraditional ways, particularly including the work of Li-Young Lee and Scott Cairns. He lives in the Peace River Watershed and walks to work.

JILL PELÁEZ BAUMGAERTNER is Professor of English and Dean of Humanities and Theological Studies at Wheaton College. She received the PhD from Emory University and has also taught at Valparaiso University. The author of five collections of poetry, including **What Cannot Be Fixed**; a textbook on poetry; a book on Flannery O'Connor; and the poetry anthology **Imago Dei**, she has also written lyrics for compositions by Richard Hillert, Carl Schalk, Michael Costello, and Daniel Kellogg. She received a Fulbright to Spain and has won many awards for her poetry. She serves as poetry editor of **The Christian Century**.

TYLER KLINE is the author of the chapbook **As Men Do Around Knives** (ELJ Publications, 2016) and the current poet laureate of Bucks County, PA. He works on a vegetable farm and teaches middle school English. His recent work is forthcoming in **the minnesota review**, **Passages North**, **Parcel**, and elsewhere. Find him online at tylerklinepoetry.com. Twitter: @tyler_kline01

ERIC POTTER is a professor of English at Grove City College (PA) where he teaches courses in modern poetry, American literature, and creative writing. His poetry has appeared in such publications as First Things, **The Christian Century**, and **Ruminate**, as well as in the anthology **Imago Dei: Poems from Christianity and Literature**. He is the author of two poetry chapbooks, **Heart Murmur and Still Life**, and a full-length collection, **Things Not Seen** (Wipf and Stock, 2015).

JACOB RIYEFF teaches literature from the early medieval through the postmodern at Marquette University. His first chapbook, Lofsangas: Poems Old and New, appeared in 2015 (Franciscan UP), and his original poems, verse translations of medieval poems, popular essays, and scholarly essays have appeared in a variety of journals and magazines. His translation of St. Æthelwold of Winchester's Old English version of the Rule of St. Benedict is forthcoming from Cistercian Publications (2017), and he is currently finishing a translation of the French poetic works of

Swami Abhishiktananda (Dom Henri Le Saux). Jacob lives on the Lower East Side of Milwaukee with his heroically patient wife and two (soon to be three!) children. jacob.riyeff@gmail.com

BARBARA CROOKER'S work has appeared in journals and anthologies such as: Christianity & Literature, The Christian Science Monitor, The Christian Century, America, Sojourners, Windhover, Perspectives, Literature and Belief, The Cresset, Tiferet, Spiritus, Ruminate, Rock & Sling, Radix, Relief, The Anglican Theological Review, The Bedford Introduction to Literature , Good Poems for Hard Times (Garrison Keillor, editor), and Looking for God in All the Right Places. Among her awards are the Thomas Merton Poetry of the Sacred Award, and she has published eight full length books of poetry, including The Book of Kells (forthcoming from Cascade Books in 2019). www.barbaracrooker.com and Twitter: @barbaracrooker

JOANNE ALLRED is the author of three poetry collections: Whetstone, which won the Flume Press Chapbook Competition, Particulate, published by Bear Star Press, and The Evolutionary Purpose of Heartbreak, recently out from Turning Point Press. She was born and grew up in Utah, but has spent most her adult life in California, where she taught for many years in the English Department at California State University, Chico.

STELLA NESANOVICH is the author of two full-length poetry collections: Vespers at Mount Angel and Colors of the River as well as four chapbooks of poems. Her poetry has appeared in many journals and magazines as well as over twenty anthologies. In 1999 she received an artist fellowship from the Louisiana Division of the Arts; in 2009 and in 2015 she was nominated for a Pushcart Prize. She is Professor Emerita of English from McNeese State University in Lake Charles, Louisiana. Her website is Nesanovich.com

DEVON MILLER-DUGGAN has published poems in Rattle, Shenandoah, Margie, Christianity and Literature, Gargoyle. She teaches Creative Writing at the University of Delaware. Her books include Pinning the Bird to the Wall in 2008 and a chapbook, Neither Prayer, Nor Bird in 2013. Alphabet Year, will be published by Wipf & Stock in 2016. devonmiller-duggan.com

AARON BROWN'S prose and poetry have been published in World Literature Today, Transition, Tupelo Quarterly, Portland Review, Ruminate, and Cimarron Review, among others. He is the author of Winnower (Wipf & Stock, 2013) and is a Pushcart Prize nominee. An MFA graduate from the University of Maryland, Aaron grew up in Chad and now lives with his wife Melinda in Sterling, Kansas, where he is an assistant professor of writing at Sterling College. www.aaronbrownwriter.com

CAMERON ALEXANDER LAWRENCE is a graduate of the University of Arizona and lives and writes in Decatur, GA, where he shares a home with his wife and three young daughters. His poems have appeared or are forthcoming in Asheville Poetry Review, Image, Pittsburgh Poetry Review, Ink & Letters, Rock & Sling, and elsewhere. cameronlawrence.com

RAINA JOINES has an MFA from the University of Florida and teaches poetry workshop, literature, and composition at the University of North Texas, where she is the faculty advisor for the North Texas Review. She is the recipient of fellowships from Blue Mountain Center, the Hambidge Center for Creative Arts and Sciences, and the Lillian E. Smith Center. She received a First Honorable Mention for her poetry from the Dana Awards in 2015, and her work is out or forthcoming in Measure, Crab Orchard Review, and Grist: The Journal for Writers.

MICHAEL D. RILEY has published six collections of poetry. The most recent, Ordinary Time: Poems for the Liturgical Year, appeared in 2016.

He has poems in two recent anthologies: Irish American Poetry From the Eighteenth Century to the Present and Blood to Remember: American Poets on the Holocaust. His poems have appeared in many periodicals, including Poetry, Poetry Ireland Review, South Carolina Review, Rattle, America, Atlanta Review, and Southern Humanities Review. He is Emeritus Professor of English from Penn State University and lives in Lancaster, PA.

BRUCE BOND is the author of fifteen books including For the Lost Cathedral (LSU, 2015), The Other Sky (Etruscan, 2015), Immanent Distance: Poetry and the Metaphysics of the Near at Hand (U of MI, 2015), Gold Bee (Crab Orchard Award, SIU, 2016), and Black Anthem (Tampa Review Prize, U of Tampa,, 2016). Two books are forthcoming: Sacrum (Four Way Books), and Blackout Starlight: New and Selected Poems (Phillabaum Award, LSU). Presently he is Regents Professor at University of North Texas.

Fiction

ROBERT MCGUILL is a four-time Pushcart
Prize nominee whose stories have appeared
in Narrative, the Southwest Review, the South
Carolina Review, American Fiction and
other publications. His short story collection,
"The Outskirts of Nowhere," was a semi-finalist
for the 2016 St. Lawrence Book Award.
Robert-McGuill.com

The Bitter Angels of Our Nature

written by ROBERT MCGUILL

Harry Stiles put down his garden rake and stood in the doorway of his shed, looking out at the pile of dead leaves in his back yard.

The country was at war again, and folks were in a lather. Everyone was clamoring for blood.

It wasn't enough we had ferreted-out and pre-emptively struck down this newest of foes, the prevailing sentiment was that we needed to crush them as well. Obliterate their seed from the planet.

"But what about the innocents?" Harry asked Charlie Dawes, his longtime neighbor, as they gabbed across the fence that afternoon. "What about the women and children?"

Charlie shrugged. "Would you have us let the bastards off, Harry? Now? When we've got our foot on their throats?" He clapped his hand on Harry's shoulder and gave with a manly smile. "Trust me, friend. It's best we take care of business while we can."

Charlie's blue-haired wife, Clarice, called to him from the back porch. "Charlie! Lunch is ready!"

Charlie glanced over his shoulder, frowning. He turned back to Harry. "If we don't address the issue now, while we're in a position of power, it's just going to come back later and bite us in the ass."

"Charlie! *Lunch!*"

Charlie glanced over his shoulder again, shaking his head. "For crying out loud. She sounds like a parrot, doesn't she? Listen, Harry, I've got to go. We'll talk about this later, all right?"

Charlie lumbered off, leaving Harry to pick up his rake and retreat to the shed. Harry had told Charlie he missed the "old days" when we settled our scores like men. He said he didn't believe in kicking a guy when he was down.

"What's happened to us, Charlie?" he said. "We used to pick people up and dust them off after we set them straight. We used to forgive and forget. When did we change? When did we become so angry?"

Charlie huffed. "You're mistaking resolve for belligerence, Harry. The world's not as simple as it used to be. We need to evolve and adapt. Move forward with the times."

"But how can we move forward if we can't let go?"

"Look, Harry, do you want to keep fighting the same battles, over and over? Because that's what happens when you take your foot off the gas. If we let go, the problem lives another day. It's that simple."

The two men argued back and forth the better part of an hour.

Harry told Charlie he feared we were becoming the very people we hated. The sort of people who enshrined their grievances. Memorialized their anger. Elevated the smallest insults to the status

THE BITTER ANGELS OF OUR NATURE

of ancient wrongs. Was that us, he asked Charlie? What that who we wanted to be?

Charlie shrugged and said we were simply coming to balance. He gave Harry a sad smile. "Harry," he said. "You're a good egg, and I like you. But you're naïve. The hard truth is, we're only doing to them what they would do to us."

Harry leaned against the door of the wooden shed. Once, when he was a kid, he sneaked into his old man's garage and fired up a wood-burning pen so he could sear his initials into his baseball glove.

He was cautious at first. But then he got carried away by the look and smell of the burning leather, and when he finished with the glove he turned the iron on a wall stud, scorching his name deep into the wood grain.

Next thing he knew, he was standing on his tiptoes atop a half-empty bucket of paint, setting fire to a cobweb. Then to an old paper bag. Finally, he torched a big black beetle hiding on a shelf near the window, which scrabbled off with its hind legs smoking.

Before he knew it, Harry had set the garage on fire. He tried to put out the flames, flapping at them wildly with a dirty rag he'd snatched from the workbench. But it did no good. The sad old shed burned to the ground.

Justice came swiftly.

Harry's old man whipped him for what he'd done, and set harsh restrictions on his personal freedoms. No visits from friends. No transistor radio to keep him company in his bedroom at night. No weekends that didn't include church, homework, and an early bedtime. His allowance? He didn't dare ask.

He spent the entire winter hating his old man, even wishing him dead. But the following spring, when his father took him out to the mill to buy lumber for a new garage, relations between them began to thaw.

During the next two months Harry and his old man worked side-by-side, rebuilding what had been destroyed. It was a long humid summer, but from the blackened foundation of the old garage fresh pine ribs began to sprout, and by the time the last nail was driven into place, miracle of miracles, Harry and his father were friends again.

The new garage, with its painted shutters and fancy flowerboxes, was a thing of beauty. Better than the old garage by a mile, though neither of them said so aloud. Harry could still remember the look on his old man's face when they'd finished. How he'd turned to Harry and clapped him on the shoulder and said, "Nice job, boy."

That afternoon Harry and his father drove out to the Dairy Queen and ate ice cream cones on a wooden bench under a shade tree. There were no lectures about the fire. No sermons about Harry having been a bad boy. No celebrations or remembrances or calls to higher ideals. There was only the fragile blue sky above them, and the clear but tacit understanding that each shared in the other's happiness.

THE BITTER ANGELS OF OUR NATURE

ANGELA DOLL CARLSON is a poet, fiction writer and essay-
ist whose work has appeared or is forthcoming in Apeiron
Review, Thin Air Magazine, Eastern Iowa Review, Whale
Road Review, St. Katherine Review, Rock and Sling, Ink
& Letters, Ruminate Magazine, Elephant Journal and Art
House America. Her memoir, "Nearly Orthodox: On Being a
Modern Woman in an Ancient Tradition" from Ancient Faith
Publishers was published in 2014. Her next book, "Garden in
the East" was released in November 2016.

Two Fathers of the Mountain

written by ANGELA DOLL CARLSON

I should not have said that I'd wished for it. I'd hoped for it, certainly, but I should not have said, "wished." She jumped on that word, pounced on it. She heard me say it though I thought I was saying it quietly, under my breath. I had hardly any breath left by then. She heard it through the storm blowing outside, the rain leaking inside, the blender running in the kitchen. *How did she hear it? How on earth did she hear it?*

She hollered from the kitchen, over the drowning sounds of the blender, the rain, the storm. It was a question, but it was not a question as much as it was a judgment, an admonition, a calling out. She thought it too, but she hoped for it. She didn't wish for it. I didn't challenge her. She knew the distinction, and so did I, but I said it aloud. That's all that matters.

He was sick and suffering. He took up space in the dining room near the bookshelves. The night before he'd asked for water. It was the middle of the night and she didn't want to get out of bed. I went. I fetched it. He wanted ice. I broke it from the metal tray. He jumped at the sound. He said he wished for it. He said it first.

The rain was a long way off and he said he saw it coming. I saw it too but I didn't say anything. He spotted the storm clouds through squinting eyes. He saw them gathering on the horizon, past the mountain range that on most days looked lonely to me. I gave them names when I was a child. They were a family there in the distance. They were inky and shadowed, two fathers, a mother and a child. One father was bigger than the other. One of the fathers was God. The mother stood a little apart from them. She was ready for heaven. She was idling there. She was too far to put her arms around the child though she wanted to. The child knew it. The fathers knew it. The bigger father had arms close enough to touch the child mountain, long enough to reach the mother mountain, to feel her fingers against his. He reached out; she reached out, there were clouds between them.

The next afternoon she saw the storm clouds. She placed buckets at the proper places. She pulled out the blender for the drinks. It would be a long night, and she wanted to be drunk for it. I watched the clouds drift in, rush in, threatening and threatening and then stalling and thundering. This was my place, to sit and wait. She rattled the buckets, but the plastic ones thudded. When the drops hit them, I anticipated the thudding. When the one metal bucket came out, I shivered. That was the sound of the taste in my mouth, aluminum and acid. There was some rust but how could it be? Where did rust happen with aluminum? That bucket she would place on top of the bookcase. I would move it to the slow drip at the baseboard closest the front door. The fall from the ceiling was longer. Gravity would make that drop stretch out so that the first sounds from that bucket would *sploosh* instead of *tink*.

TWO FATHERS OF THE MOUNTAIN

She couldn't hear the difference.

When we ran out of ice, she scraped it from the bottom of the freezer. We didn't care by then except that it gave her a reason to complain to me about the ice trays. They were always empty, she said. It was so easy to fill them, she told me. I didn't use the ice, only the small sliver that came from that metal tray, the one that made him jump. She said it must be the ghosts, using up all the ice. I didn't argue. She might be half right about that. There were ghosts here. They were all about being empty, feeling empty, making empty, except when it rained and then they were all about the buckets filling from those leaking places. Protect the books, she'd say-shout from the kitchen. I put the plastic bucket up there, and she saw it. She didn't know why it mattered, but it did matter.

His breathing was shallow, jagged, like it was running through a fan on the way out. I watched his chest rise and fall. I whispered to him about the mountain, about the rain coming, about the drops in buckets. I stroked his head with just the tips of my fingers. His gray hair was greasy now, plastered to his head after the heavy sweat from a long broken fever. She would go through his things in the evening when she thought I was asleep. There was nothing left of him, save for the house and that bit of land that no one could farm. She'd leave when he was gone. I'd stay there until the house fell down around me and then maybe I'd go to the mountains. I whispered this to him. I reached my arms around his body, still warm to the touch. I lowered my face to him, hovered just above his open lips, turned my head, closed my eyes, and let his breath press against my cheek. The air carried a laugh-like sound from deep in his lungs– *huh huh huh.*

She came in from the kitchen, one drink in each hand. She said heard me under my breath speaking; she called it muttering, but it wasn't so much muttering. I just didn't have much breath left by then. The clouds were covering the mountains, the two fathers and the child, the mother reaching and pulling back, thundering, blender now quiet in the kitchen, the drops falling hard from the sky, filling the gutters, filling the craters, filling the aging wood with cracks where the wishes would be. It would not be long now.

SAINT KATHERINE COLLEGE

An Independent Orthodox
Christian College
of Liberal Arts and Sciences

North San Diego County

"Inquiry Seeking Wisdom"

- Challenging Academics
- Interdisciplinary Curriculum
- 12:1 Student:Professor Ratio
- Small Class Size
- Orthodox Christian Worldview
- Beautiful Campus Location

www.skcca.edu
760.471.1316

Non-Fiction

MARJORIE MADDOX is a Sage Graduate Fellow of Cornell University (MFA) and Professor of English and Creative Writing at Lock Haven University. She has published eleven collections of poetry—including True, False, None of the Above—the short story collection What She Was Saying (2017 Fomite), and over 450 stories, essays, and poems in journals and anthologies. Co-editor of Common Wealth: Contemporary Poets on Pennsylvania, she also has published two children's books with many forthcoming.

Taking Refuge

written by MARJORIE MADDOX

The sixty-year-old volunteer in a coyote T-shirt wipes the sweat from her brow with a brown bandana, and then turns to us. "This morning at 10:00 am," she says, "there were 50 people on this tour."

It is almost 2:00 pm and nearing 100 degrees. There are only four of us waiting on two paint-peeling benches. My daughter and I look around at the large, faded sign and near-empty lot, which we passed twice before deciding if we had reached the entrance to our destination. "I guess this is it," I said just fifteen minutes earlier, as I pulled alongside a still-locked gate. A smaller sign read, "Tour starts here." A minute later, an elderly man in jeans had strolled out, smiled, unlocked the padlock, and swung wide the gate.

Since my eighteen-year-old had slept until noon, we couldn't venture out until now into the hot sun for the second and last tour of the day. We are joined only by a sporty grandmother and her pre-teen grandson, who is visiting her from California. They have hit the local amusement park they tell us, and tomorrow they will hike under the waterfalls in the nearby state park. Today, though, today is animal refuge day. The grandmother, who is younger than I am, shields her eyes from the sun and nods towards us. "Want some cold water?" she offers.

"Yeah, sure!" I exclaim, and she retrieves a bottle from the cooler in her nearby SUV.

"To Cats of the World!" we toast.

In a sense, my daughter is on vacation as well. At home for a week from her pre-college summer job a few hours away, she has been joining me for day excursions, impromptu adventures in between medical appointments that brought her back to our suburban Pennsylvania home before she begins college classes. "This will be great, Mom," she says as we pull away from the dentist's office, the GPS on her iPhone now set to "T & D's Cats of the World: Animal Refuge Specializing in Exotic Felines and Wildlife."

And so she and I, the animal lovers in the family, are off on a last hurrah to explore a 35-acre wild animal refuge way off the beaten path in our segment of the state. The site has been open since 1985, but we only just learned of this place, and—although we have ventured out as tourists—we are surprised to find we are not at a tourist attraction, but at someone's expanded home, a home that has been opened up to over 200 animals that have been abused, rejected, abandoned, or in some other way mistreated.

The elderly owners' adult daughter, one of the children who has taken over the day-to-day management of the refuge, appears with feed bucket in hand, quickly introduces herself, then turns back to her chores. She nods goodbye to the guide.

I look at my daughter, who is looking at me. "Kinda cool," I tilt my head and whisper, "It's just you, me, and them."

We take another swig of water and are on our way—a volunteer guide, a grandmother and her grandson, my daughter and I—for an hour walk over the property and into the lives of the animals, the owners, our small group, and—yes—even ourselves.

They come from circuses, zoos, government agencies, people's apartments—these lions, tigers, bobcats, but also bear, fox, lemurs, monkeys, parrots, and other creatures. Almost immediately, our guide tears up. She has been driving here twice a week from the next small town over for twenty years. Her tears show it continues to change her life. As she points out the spider monkeys, she tells us about the pet primate that was dressed up and treated like a baby, the raccoon that was fed primarily candy, and the black bear that was chained for years in a man's front yard. "What's the matter with people?" my daughter leans over and asks. What, indeed?

Near each animal is a sign that lists its donors, who are contributing to that animal's food and care. "If it could," I ask my daughter, "what would that otter write on the sign about its own life?"

My daughter counters, "What, if it could talk, would that skunk tell us?" We giggle, but our questions also are serious. What, we wonder, have the rescued animals learned from the strict teacher of experience?

While we stare in the eyes of a particularly mischievous monkey, I think of the TV commercials for sponsoring wide-eyed, thin-boned orphans. Yet, though many of this refuges' animals arrived scared, malnourished, and/or with bones broken, today they are lazing in the sun, scurrying up and down ramps, swinging from tires, or hiding in the vast expanse of tall grasses. Our guide looks on admiringly. I don't ask if she has children of her own; clearly she has "adopted" several of the "grown-up kids" at Cats of the World.

It is the hottest day of the summer, but my daughter, who hated any family vacations that forced her too long in the sun for "educational" tours, is mesmerized. She squints in the bright light to read each creature's story. The names, we learn, are only known by the owners and volunteers, whose relationship with each allows them to best care for their adopted clan. They, alone, have earned this communication. Visitors calling out bears' monikers, whistling loudly to the Macaws, throwing bread at the coatis—none of this is allowed, and for good reason, the guide explains. Animals' well being over entertainment is the mantra. Diverse places to hide from spectators allow animals the choice of whether or not to be "on display."

"These animals are wild, wild, wild," the volunteer reminds us again and again. She waves her arms for emphasis. "They are not—and never should be—"pets."" I think of our local SPCA and, even there, of all the returned Christmas presents of rabbits, cats, and dogs—animals that turned out to be too much work for a very young child or a very busy family. But here, on this family plot turned sanctuary, over 200 creatures leap or growl or splash in a safe environment. If we listen closely to their healing, what will we hear about ourselves?

On our windy path down dirt roads and around wooded bends, it becomes increasingly obvious that such consistent and safe care of so many is a lifetime of hard work. "Whoa," the grandmother walking alongside us jokes when she sees the expanse of the property, "What kind of allowance did their kids earn growing up?"

My daughter rolls her eyes. "Nothing, I'm sure."

I wonder at what moment the owners decided to commit their lives, and in turn their family's lives, to the nurture not of a few goldfish, guinea pigs, or hamsters, but to this diverse fur-and-feather community. Some parrots, we're told by the tall and rather cute grandson, live 60-80 years. "80 years!" my daughter and I exclaim in unison. Eighteen years of raising my daughter zoom past. Eighteen years of preparing her to "fly the nest." Multiply that by almost four and a half—not exactly a passing fancy.

Soon, however, we find out that Cats of the World wasn't a one-moment decision at all. Instead, it was a series of small choices that snowballed. It began, the volunteer tells us, when the father, Terry (the "T" in "T and D's Cats of the World") took in injured wildlife discovered by locals. An avid animal lover, he nursed the creatures back to health, then returned them to the wild. Later, when he rescued cougars

TAKING REFUGE

and bobcats from illegal sales, the word spread. Here was an individual helping abandoned and abused animals. Calls came in from around Pennsylvania, from neighboring states, and then from even farther away. Cats of the World, which started out with wild cats but now hosts much more, unfurled into the homegrown refuge that it is today.

As we walk along, my daughter and I talk about how—day in and day out— the owners communicate to the animals through action. The fox darting in and out of its man-made den doesn't bark its gratitude, but it knows its food comes on a long pole through the fence. The brown bear scratching against a tree knows that someone will clean and refill the small swimming pool of water he uses on especially hot days. What really grips us is how many of the animals were captives their entire lives; they can survive no longer on their own in the wild. Others are too weak. Some are rescued birthday entertainment, "photo animals" that were too expensive to keep and would otherwise be put to sleep. We try to look in their eyes, but they are too fast, too quick, too busy with their animal lives to heed us. Their communication is made of furtive stuff.

The owners' wooded trail provides respite from the heat, so we take another gulp of water and continue with our five-some past wolves, coyotes, lions, and leopards. Our companions, the grandmother and grandson (whose names we never learn) point at a yawning tiger and share a joke about an uncle. My daughter and I marvel at the lanky and beautiful servals, which pay us no mind. They are too busy slinking past each other, communicating in some way with their own family.

What we also see throughout our trek is the owners' family. In the background or off to the side, they are sloshing out food, cleaning pens, mowing fields, repairing animal "playgrounds," and building new shelters. Like their charges, they also pay us no mind—that is, until we ask about the animals. The creatures' habits, food source, life span: the owner's daughter is an especially rich source of information.

The last time I see her, I have one more question. "How," I ask her as she refills a water trough for the Binturong , "do you ever go on vacation?"

She looks at me as if the idea has never occurred to her. "Well," she says, continuing on with her work, "we don't." Then she heads back to a small cart for a shovel. "If I have to be away for a day, I just call my brother. He knows all our routines. But I don't need to call him often."

On the last leg of our educational hike, we stop to see the parrots—all sixty or so. In huge cages, some are huddled together in twos or threes as if conspiring ways to save the world. Others flap from one branch to another in great paintbrush strokes of reds, greens, blues, and yellows. A few, perched alone and aloof, peer out at us: the families displayed on the other side of the bars.

Social creatures, almost all of the birds are singing. Some are even talking. A Blue Fronted Amazon blurts out what could be "What's up, pussycat?" but sounds more like "Wasp at?" My daughter takes out her iPhone and begins filming.

As we finish our journey, my daughter and I bid adieu to the birds and thanks and farewell to our traveling companions. We toss our water bottle in the supplied bin, thank the grandmother again for the drink, and—for the drive home—buy another bottle from the small but well-stocked gift store. Cranking up the air conditioning in our Elantra, we head back to our almost-quiet and cooler home an hour away.

There Gizmo, the lineolated parakeet that has traveled home with my daughter while her boyfriend vacations with his extended family, whistles his loud Welcome Home song. Automatically, my daughter translates: "I missed you! I missed you!"

We do our best to whistle back: short, loud bursts, then quiet, breathy ones. It is the rhythm of our communication. After a few minutes, we open the cage and let him fly around the room. When he settles on my daughter's head, we take turns telling Gizmo the tale of our day. I wonder what, in his smart bird brain, he will think. I wonder what he already knows. About us. About the world. About cats.

TAKING REFUGE

MARYANNE WILIMEK lives in Minnesota where she spends as much time as possible out-of-doors. Her poetry and creative nonfiction have appeared in The Gettysburg Review, Choice Magazine Listening audio anthology, Ars Medica, Big Muddy, Relief, Lake Country Journal, Radix and elsewhere.

May I Borrow Your Story?

written by MARYANNE WILIMEK

I give rides to strangers. This is how it started. It's winter in northern Minnesota. I am driving home from a grocery store on a Wednesday afternoon when I see an elderly man in a tan parka standing alone at a corner bus stop. His shoulders are raised against a bitter wind; his chin is buried deep in his neck scarf. My heart sighs as a narrative takes off in my head:

> He lost his beloved wife four years ago and each morning he still struggles with what it means to get out of bed. To put on shoes. To eat a bowl of cornflakes. Today he is up early because the pain

in his lower left molar is unbearable. The dentist had a cancella-tion and could fit him in this afternoon, so now he waits at the bus stop, shivering, and each time he inhales, the frigid air slams his tender tooth like a ball-peen hammer. He wraps a frayed knit scarf tighter around his cheeks.

I circle the block. He is still there.

They took away his driver's license two years ago, about the same time his 1986 Buick sedan finally refused to go into gear. Six weeks passed before he could bring himself to call a tow truck to haul it to the junkyard. The morning he heard the truck beeping and backing up into his driveway, he retreated to his basement where, with shaky, thick-knuckled fingers, he spent several hours sorting piles of old nails and screws into empty peanut butter jars.

I pull up to the bus stop and buzz down the passenger-side window. "You must be freezing," I shout against the wind. "I'm heading down-town and could give you a ride." We only have one bus line in this little town, so I know that's where he's going.

He looks down the block—the bus is nowhere in sight. He comes close to the car window. "Well, that would be nice, if it's not too much trouble." He gets into the car. "I need to pick up a few groceries." I help him click the seat belt. "The grandkids are coming over tonight and the wife wants to make spaghetti and brownies."

So this isn't a tragic story. A wife and grandkids are a part of this old man's life and I am happy to hear it. I drop him off at the store, lie to him about "having to stay in town to run errands," and insist on com-ing back to pick him up. Better to stretch the truth than try to convince a stranger that he is worth twenty minutes of my time.

"That would be nice, if it's not too much trouble," he says.

Several months later I notice an elderly woman sitting on one of two metal folding chairs at the front of the same grocery store. A shop-ping cart holding her packed plastic bags is parked next to her. She is still there when I come to the checkout line fifteen minutes later. As I unload my cart, the cashier calls over to her, "You doing okay, Emma?"

The aching in Emma's hips was nearly unbearable. She had no choice but to sit on this hard, metal chair and wait for the bus. As she shifted her weight, she closed her eyes in a quiet moan of pain. She looked at her groceries—how would she get them up the stairs and into the house this time? Once again she would have to call on her daughter-in-law Grace, a sad and bitter woman who never missed the chance to impress upon Emma just how inconvenient Emma's needs had become. No one had ever been so inappropriately named as Grace.

I smile at the cashier. "Is she waiting for a ride?"

"For nearly an hour. It's that new on-demand city bus system...makes these folks wait so long." She hands me my receipt. "I hope she doesn't have ice cream in one of those bags."

I approach the old woman. "Would you like a ride home? I'd be happy to give you one."

Her face brightens. "Oh...but I live five miles out, west of town..."

"That's just the direction I'm headed." Better to stretch the truth than try to convince a stranger that she is worth a detour.

"That would be nice."

Although I am happy she takes me up on my offer, I am bothered by her instant trust. She should be more wary.

We arrive at her big farmhouse, a place she says she shares with two unmarried adult sons who are out doing whatever it is farmers do on late spring afternoons. She picks up one bag, I take the other two, and as I watch her walk up the gravel path in front of me I can't help but think of those slow Italian grandmothers in sensible shoes that I had watched carry market bags up cobblestone streets in Umbrian hill towns like Gubbio and Montefalco. Emma has that same kind of old-world sturdiness. We enter a back screen door and come into a kitchen filled with the warm smells of baking. She puts her bag on a counter and takes two oatmeal-raisin cookies off a sheet of waxed paper. She presses the cookies into my hand. They are big and soft and fragrant with cinnamon, like my mother used to make.

I know it's my mother's doing that I like giving rides to older people. Mom was born in 1918 and grew up at the tail end of an era when many women never bothered to get a driver's license. Her parents never owned a car, and as long as my dad was alive my mother had no problems with transportation since they went most places together: church, volunteer work at St. Vincent de Paul, visits to the grandkids, appointments at the dentist, the optometrist—and later on—the oncologist, the cardiologist, the surgeon. After Dad died, Mom had to rely on relatives for transportation, as the city had no reliable cab service and she was far too poor of both eyesight and balance to cope with a public bus. Access to a once- or twice-weekly ride was all she needed to stay in her own home—and she most desperately wanted to stay in her own home. She once confided in me how much she disliked asking for rides, how much she disliked the thought of inconveniencing people.

> Dolores was a considerate woman who genuinely hated to put people out. She kept a list of names and numbers in a drawer by the phone: her four sons, her one brother, an unmarried sister-in-law, a married sister-in-law. She kept meticulous track of who gave her rides and when, intent as she was on spreading the burden around as thinly as possible.

I was living and working in a small city six hundred miles away from my mom, and whenever I went back to visit her I took at least a week's worth of vacation time. I would tell her to save up as many errands as she could, and then allow me to be her chauffer. These would be the times she would not only schedule medical appointments, but also take care of less essential tasks, like a trip to the laundromat to wash blankets and throw rugs, or to the drug store to choose birthday cards for each of her twenty-three grandkids.

My parents are both deceased now. I have two elderly aunts who live in the same city my parents did, and I bless the thoughtfulness of in-town relatives who get them to where they need to go. I compensate

MAY I BORROW YOUR STORY?

for my absence by offering rides to other people's aunts and mothers and grandpas. I take them to the doctor, the dentist, the hairdresser, the barber. It pleases me to think that someone's grandmother doesn't have to leave the clinic with an appointment card in hand wondering how in the world she will get back there next week for her lab test. I found a local nonprofit agency that coordinates volunteers like me with people who need rides, which means my opportunities to help are no longer left to a chance encounter at a bus stop.

I've met an interesting assortment of people over the years. Sometimes, while I wait in the car or the doctor's office, I unwittingly dream up fictional sketches based on initial encounters. Other times, if I get to know them better, I find that their real lives are far more compelling. A woman I'll call "Shirley" lived thirty miles out in the country and is the only person I've ever known to talk without punctuation.

> She merged one thought into the next and the next and without a break she would go from Ernie-the-one-armed-handyman who she watched clear her driveway of five inches of snow to her son Denny who drives a van-for-hire whistles Sousa tunes and lives somewhere near a military base she thought it was a Navy base in Alabama to the nice Jehovah Witness ladies who used to try and convert her but now just come to visit to her dog Little Stinker who is crazy for Burger King onion rings and who has bloodied her linoleum more than once by dragging in a dead baby bunny before she could stop him…

It was a *very* long ride, taking Shirley to the clinic and back.

I drove "Eleanor" to a hair appointment every week for several months. For a woman who appeared to be over ninety, Eleanor had impeccable posture. Her clothes and makeup were imbued with a faded elegance reminiscent of Katherine Hepburn. She drew jet-black brows above her eyes, the same way she had done for years, no doubt, before her hair went gray, then white. But now she drew the eyebrows on with a shaky hand and it had the effect of making her look perpetually surprised.

One day, completely out of the blue, she told me she used to pilot a ski plane to deliver U.S. mail to desolate areas in northern Minnesota in the 1940s. Now it was my turn to look surprised. As much as I loved this startling, proto-feminist image of Eleanor as a young Amelia Earhart, I was more than a little skeptical of her memories. I asked her a few quasi-technical questions about piloting, questions to which I knew the answers. To my sweet surprise, Eleanor never skipped a beat. She responded factually, and then added some nerve-racking stories of mid-flight stalls and emergency snowfield landings that left no doubt in my mind that her stories were true. It was about eight months after the last time I saw her that I read her obituary in the newspaper. It was a very brief account of a very long life, and it never mentioned ski planes.

The first time I was called to drive "Florence," I realized I had been to her place before. Her yard had been a stop on a local garden tour, and I remembered her flowerbeds as lovely studies in controlled chaos, exuberant in a "constrained anarchy" kind of way. But that was twenty years prior. Florence was now in her 80s, and it was apparent that age had pulled tight the boundaries of her life. Her yard was smothered in weeds and wild vines; a scattering of Black-eyed Susans was all that evidenced the much-loved gardens that once grew here. I read Florence's obituary about three months later, in late fall, and I thought of the Black-eyed Susans and how they would be brittle and gone to seed, dusted with the season's first snow.

When I first met "Marnie" she was waiting for me, sitting on a chair just inside the door to her apartment building. When I offered her my arm, she took it. As we walked to my car I slowed my pace to match her short, unsteady steps. In the clinic waiting room we sat in silence, side by side. I offered to get her a magazine, but she declined. The nurse called her name and I stood to again offer her my arm, which again she took. Then she asked if I would mind coming into the exam room with her, a request that made me feel both privileged and unprepared: the role of advocate was usually reserved for a relative or close friend.

In the sterile space of the exam room, while waiting for the doctor, she calmly confided in me about the cervical cancer, the unexpected drug interactions, the unexplained problems with stents, the ineffective chemo treatments.

I could tell by the way the doctor interacted with Marnie that he knew courage when he saw it. He also knew trouble when he saw it, and, after the exam, he told Marnie that she needed to check into the hospital that day. The nurse offered her a wheelchair to get back to my car and she accepted. She told me she had a feeling this might happen and had packed a small bag that morning with some of her things. Could I take her to the hospital? *Yes.* Could we first stop by her place to pick up her bag? *Of course.* As I pulled into the parking lot of her apartment building, she said she'd prefer to wait in the car. She gave me her key and apartment number, and told me I would see a number of yellow sticky-notes posted on the inside of her door, all with pre-written messages. I was to find the one that said "Hospital" and stick it to the front of her door, so her neighbors would know why she wouldn't be answering her buzzer.

Her apartment was easy to find—a yellow note reading "Clinic" was stuck on the outside of the door. Inside, I found her black zippered bag on the hall floor just where she said it would be. I picked it up, and then I stood for just a moment and took notice of the things that were Marnie's. The framed pictures of grandchildren on her end table. The well-stocked, floor-to-ceiling bookshelf. The piece of unfinished knitting resting on the arm of the couch. Three African violets on the windowsill, all on white china saucers, all in purple bloom. As I turned to leave I scanned the twenty or so sticky-notes on the back of her door: "Dining Room," "Bridge at Sylvia's," "Church," "Grocery Store," "Bible Study" "Physical Therapy" "Hospital." In spite of the upheavals of her devastating illness, I had the sense that this woman knew exactly where she was—and where she was going—with or without her sticky-notes. I exchanged "Clinic" for "Hospital" on the front of her door and locked it behind me.

The weight of Marnie's weariness was clear, and when we arrived at the hospital I told her to wait in the car until I returned with a wheelchair. Her doctor had called ahead, so she was able to breeze through admissions with a quick signature. Once we were in her room, she asked me to open her bag and hang a few clothes in the closet. Her slippers she wanted on the floor by the bed. A red rubber band bound together an address book and a well-worn black prayer book; she wanted them on the nightstand. I sat with her for a few moments, asked if there was anything else she needed. Then I did something I typically didn't do—I wrote my home phone number on a piece of hospital notepaper and slipped it under the rubber band. I told her to call me directly when she needed a ride back home, so she wouldn't have to go through the volunteer coordinator. A couple days passed and she didn't call. Then I saw her obituary.

I am grateful that I had the privilege of offering Marnie—and others like her—this one simple measure of dignity: the independence of personal transportation, the courtesy of a car door held open and gently closed, the offer of meeting an unspoken need: *As long as we're out and about, are there any other errands you need to run? The post office? The grocery store? It's no trouble, really.* I think of my mother as she aged, and I remember the increasing physical and psychological effort it took just to get dressed, go out the door, and get into a car. *Is there anything you need to pick up at the drug store?*

I keep the image of Marnie's apartment in my journal—her purple African violets, her knitting, her bookshelf—and I can't help but think it would please her to know that someone remembers her this way.

> The volunteer driver waited inside the door as the widow took a key from a blue ceramic bowl—a bowl her husband bought for her years ago on a trip they took to Umbria in Italy. Her winter coat was resting on the arm of a recliner, and she took care in putting it on, knowing how the heavy wool weighed down on her tender shoulder bones. As they stepped into the hallway, she turned and pressed a yellow sticky-note to the front of her door. "A trick I learned—lets my neighbors know where I am," she said, as she turned the key.

MAY I BORROW YOUR STORY?

MARY ANNE REESE has written two poetry chapbooks, Down Deep and Raised by Water, both from Finishing Line Press. Her essays and poems have appeared in magazines and newspapers including America, St. Anthony Messenger, Sojourners, and The Cincinnati Enquirer. In 1998, her poem "Triduum" won the Catholic Press Association's first place award for best poetry. She holds advanced degrees in law and, more recently, in theology (Xavier University) and English (Northern Kentucky University).

Anhinga Time

written by MARY ANNE REESE

During a hard time in my life, I sit and stare at the Anhinga. The bird is perched beside a canal that winds through a Sarasota golf course. I am perched on a gliding chair on a lanai. In this hot May, no one else is around.

The slender bird stands tall on stilt legs with its wings stretched out some four feet. It never moves. Except for the Anhinga's dark elegance, it could be a scarecrow back home in an Ohio field.

My pale, inelegant body fills the patio chair. I too am still, except for occasionally sweeping the woods, the lagoon and the greens with my binoculars. Four large turtles sun on a rock; their black shells glisten and overlap. A great blue heron wades into the water. A baby eagle teeters on the edge of its nest, a mature one soars overhead. The eagle's screech pierces the air.

The morning sun shines bright and a breeze ripples through the Anhinga's feathers. I can see each individual black and silver feather dangle from the wing. I can also see the green grass through spaces between the feathers.

*

Earlier in the week, I saw a long thin neck protruding from the canal. I jumped back, sure it was a snake. Then I noticed the beak. I watched for a while, perplexed. The head submerged and the bird surfaced several yards away, pointed its beak at the sky and swallowed hard. Then it submerged, surfaced and swallowed again. Within a few minutes, it had taken its fishing expedition down the canal and out of sight. I was impressed: this bird works hard. Later, I looked it up in a field guide: the Anhinga.

*

The Anhinga's swim reminds me of the races I swam at our swim club growing up: "Let's see who can swim the farthest underwater." I prepared by gulping deep breaths. I then took a long shallow dive, opened my eyes to a stinging blur and kicked like mad. My arms pulled down along my sides and then back up again. I always won the race. I wasn't fast, but I could stay underwater forever.

*

I am still swimming underwater. For ten years, I have been responsible for both my parents. I am their only child. One after another, each has developed Alzheimer's.

My father died five years ago and nightmare images still visit me in sleep. His gaunt face and blank stare. The hospital sheet he stuffed

ANHINGA TIME

into his mouth after lunch. A shaking hand reaching out of his grave. I shudder at all I could not do to save him.

*

The Anhinga takes a couple of steps with its webbed feet and turns to face the sun. I move my chair a few inches out of the shade.

*

I have just moved my mother to her fourth home in ten years. The move has cost her memory. Each day I call her after supper.

"When are you coming to see me?" is always her first question, even if have visited that same day. I've memorized a script to help me not to feel.

"Soon, Mom. Have you got your buttons?"

Silence. "Oh, here they are." Silence again. "No, that's for the bed. . . Oh, here."

"Mom, point your buttons at the TV and press nine. The shows you like are coming on." She enjoys the nightly broadcasts of "Jeopardy" and "Wheel of Fortune."

A high-pitched tone sounds in my ear.

"Mom, you pressed nine on the phone, not the remote. Let's try again. Do you see the little black box with numbers on it?"

"Oh, I'm not myself today," her voice drops. "I don't know what I'm doing."

"That's okay, Mom," I try to sound upbeat. "You remember the important things. Now we can do this—let's try again."

"Honey, I better go. I don't feel good right now."

"Okay," I finally acquiesce. "I love you, Mom."

I hear her weak response, "I love you. What would I ever do without you?"

I wince and then hear a click.

*

A sparrow lands close to the Anhinga. It seems microscopic in the tall bird's shadow. The sparrow leaves. The Anhinga never moves.

*

I have also been also swimming underwater at work. Each day, I sit in a downtown office surrounded by prison-gray walls. My windows look out on gray air. In this six-month period, Ohio has had a year's worth of rain.

The criminal justice system never slows down. My inbox overflows; deadlines are always imminent. I try working weekends to catch up. The building ventilation is off, the air close and stale. In the isolation, I sometimes manage to piece together a short memo or perhaps cut and paste from something else created in more energetic times. But the in-box never disappears or even shrinks. I end up staring at my computer screen until it blurs.

Each night after work, I return to the home where I live alone. On the front stoop are jagged pieces of rubber that once fit together as a welcome mat. I come in the front door and slip upstairs without turning on a light. I don't want to see the dust that coats the tables or the wine stains on the carpet. I don't want to see the unfolded laundry strewn across the loveseat. I don't want to see the draining board covered with unopened bills. I simply want to crawl into bed. With luck and a pill, I may fall asleep.

*

The Anhinga still stands motionless on the dam. Unlike a duck, the Anhinga has no glandular oils to waterproof its feathers. This deficit is a mixed blessing. Without the oil coating, the bird can stay underwater longer. Yet, nothing rolls off its back. The Anhinga absorbs everything it touches. After it swims awhile, its feathers become waterlogged and it starts to sink. At that point, the Anhinga flies low if it can fly at all.

I too lack the natural ability to let things slide off my back. I hold every moment, every image, every word. More than anything, I

ANHINGA TIME

hold pain. Even as I sit here on the lanai, recent images run through my mind.

—The blue-eyed killer who sits across the table from me, and the guards who stand on either side of him.

—The parolee who screams through my phone, "You're a fucking liar."

—The email that begins, "I am deeply disappointed that you failed..."

—My mother's question: "Why do I have to move?"

I hold such moments in my body the same way the Anhinga holds water in its feathers. A bitter taste coats my throat. Stomach pain sometimes doubles me over. I toss and turn at 4 a.m. with the same *what-ifs* running over and over through my brain. What if I can't find a place for my Mom? What if I can't pay these bills? What if I lose my job?

What if I don't?

I am drenched and I am foundering.

*

"Why can't you work?" the psychologist asks. He pushes back in his recliner and strokes his beard. A clipboard rests in his lap.

I sit on the edge of an overstuffed sofa, eye level with a cut-out of Geordi LaForge mounted on his file drawer. A life-sized Klingon with a braided forehead menaces in the corner while a plastic model of the Starship Enterprise hangs from the ceiling. From the lobby, I can still hear the boombox blaring Kansas' "To the Point of Know Return." I should be thinking *What the hell*? I should be laughing out loud or fleeing this room. Instead, I sit here stammering,

"I can't—I can't concentrate. I have these dark thoughts . . ."

He cuts me off. "Do you know who the President is?"

"Barack."

"The vice-president?"

A litany of skits from Saturday Night Live runs through my mind until I finally picture teeth.

"Biden."

"What does your house look like right now?"

I tell him.

The doctor gives me a list of colors and then reads me a story. After the story, he asks me to repeat the list of colors. The only one I recall is brown.

He asks me to count backward from one hundred by sevens. He stops me at sixty-five. "What are the dark thoughts you say you have?"

"Sometimes, instead of watching my mother disappear one brain cell at a time, I want to disappear into the woods."

"I know," he says at last. "My dad died of Alzheimer's." He looks down and touches his eye. I lean my head back. My breathing slows.

"Your reaction is normal," the doctor goes on. "Soldiers come home from war suffering from post-traumatic stress, but you don't even get the 'post.' You're still in the war." At these words, I want to curl up on the sofa and cry.

"I'm going to recommend that you be off for at least a month. That will give you time to get some rest and move your mother." I am bewildered and relieved.

*

The next day, I awaken with no place I have to be, nothing I have to do, no guaranteed contact with any human being. My speed has shifted from ninety to zero. I am terrified.

My doctor has prescribed antidepressants. Instead of putting me to sleep as other medicines do, this one leaves me shaking with fever, clenching my jaw, too nauseous to eat. For a week, I can't get out of bed. Although I love to read, I can't even reach for a book. I spend hours staring at the wall.

Is this madness? I wonder. Will it last forever? Will I end up living under a bridge?

The drug wears off, the symptoms abate and I try again. Same result.

"You can't take medicine—you're a wuss," my doctor teases. She suggests that I can get the same result through exercise.

Although I've always loved bicycling and swimming, I haven't found time. All winter and spring, I have gone to work in the dark

ANHINGA TIME

and come home in the dark. Although my life has been frenetic these past years, most of it has been spent sitting. Behind a desk, behind the wheel, beside a sickbed. My body has stalled out while my brain was in overdrive.

Each morning, I tell myself that the most important thing I can do today is move. I bicycle twenty-three miles. I walk three miles in the mall. I soak in a hot bath. As I move my body more, my thoughts slow down.

*

A few weeks into this program, a friend invites me to meet her in Sarasota. She texts me a video of sunset, with waves lapping the sand. Waves, sand, sun—three things Ohio lacks. I book a flight.

In Florida, I meet the Anhinga. Each morning, it stands in the same place on a dam, its wings stretched out. I watch the bird for an hour, longer. It rarely moves. It allows the slow work of the sun and breeze to dry its every feather.

The Anhinga knows how to be still; its life depends on it. Stillness restores the Anhinga. Then it flies, swims, and fishes once more.

*

I do not know how to be still. I can't even sit still in front of a TV. For relaxation, I take graduate courses, open multiple screens on my laptop, and make road trips. I drench myself in activity with no way to let it evaporate from my system. Not even briefly.

Deep down, I don't really believe that stillness is allowed me. I also have to admit that I fear stillness. If I keep moving, maybe I can save my mother. If I keep moving, maybe I can rescue all these work projects. If I keep moving, maybe I can stave off illness and death and leap tall buildings. Constant action holds my fear at bay; it keeps me from facing all I am not.

*

One of my frequent driving destinations is a Trappist monastery in Kentucky. Sometimes I drive for several hours simply to attend night prayer, and then turn around and come home. I am drawn to the monks' silence even as I can't stand my own. I appreciate how they rarely leave their enclosure even though I can't stay home. I love watching them turn to face the icon of Mary, each one dark and still as the Anhinga. All of us stand motionless in the chapel while two flames flicker in the night.

Some mysterious treasure wells up in the monks from the silence and stillness, and sometimes it spills over into words. Recently, I heard a monk conclude his sermon by asking, "Dare we be still enough to know the closeness of God? To allow the divine to pervade our being, take hold of our consciousness, become the very source of all we love and desire?"

*

Dare I?

I have spent these last weeks asking that question. Now I look out at the Anhinga standing still on the dam. While I watch, all manner of wildlife crosses my view. Geckos, turtles, rosiette spoonbills. Blue herons, sand hill cranes, frogs. Some teach me. The snake leaves behind its dead skin. What part of myself needs to be shed? The baby eagle finally steps from the nest and soars. Can I trust my wings again?

*

Most of all, I learn from the Anhinga, with its life balanced between tireless work and stillness. My life has not been balanced at all. No wonder I am drowning.

I leave Sarasota less pale after soaking in the sun. I leave with muscles that feel taut from walking and swimming in the Gulf. I leave with my mind clearer after moving my body and then sitting still in a world of birds, reptiles and plants. My racing what-ifs have slowed. Sometimes they even stop.

ANHINGA TIME

The Anhinga works with a fury and then it stands still. I come home to Ohio and try to do the same. I tap on the keyboard writing poetry into the night. I walk the perimeter of an old wooden basketball court thirty-three times. I sit at an overlook and watch the Ohio River flow across our valley as it has for centuries.

I call my mother and answer hard questions until a time when she can no longer pick up the phone. Sometimes I lie awake with my heart racing, lamenting all that has changed so fast, worrying over all that might come. Picturing the big shorebird, however, helps me to lie still and breathe deeply.

I want to live in Anhinga time.

From the Editor

by FR KALEEG HAINSWORTH

'Turning and turning in the widening gyre
The falcon cannot hear the falconer;
Things fall apart; the centre cannot hold;
Mere anarchy is loosed upon the world,
The blood-dimmed tide is loosed, and everywhere
The ceremony of innocence is drowned;
The best lack all conviction, while the worst
Are full of passionate intensity...'

These are the chilling first lines lines of 'The Second Coming' written by WB Yeats in 1920. The 'widening gyre' he describes is a world increasingly disconnected from its origins and spinning ever outward into disillusion. We may argue about the origins and debate the solutions, but there is no escaping the reality that we today face a momentous time in human history. Climate change, exponential population expansion, shifting geo-politics, and polarized thinking are just a few of the challenges we face now. This is a moment of truth for us humans, and like all such moments it requires a poet.

I have accepted the position of Editor of St Katherine Review with humility and with a mandate. I believe poetry is a celebration of truth in words and that a poet practices daily the discipline of seeing purely. As editor, I know my mandate, at a time such as this, is to help St Katherine Review become a vibrant, strong, and rigorous platform for the poets of our age to speak truth and beauty to the world. I am calling out now for you - the poets, the writers, the courageous 'unacknowledged legislators of the world' (as Shelly called you) - to call back with your verses and your beauty and your truth. Send me your best. St Katherine's Review will honour it, and you, and your vocation.

Made in the USA
San Bernardino, CA
07 February 2017